ALMOST HUMAN

Previous winners of the Dorset Prize

Ice, Mouth, Song by Rachel Contreni Flynn
Selected by Stephen Dunn

Red Summer by Amaud Jamaul Johnson
Selected by Ray Gonzalez

Dancing in Odessa by Ilya Kaminsky
Selected by Eleanor Wilner

Dismal Rock by Davis McCombs
Selected by Linda Gregerson

Biogeography by Sandra Meek
Selected by the Tupelo Press Editors

Archicembalo by G. C. Waldrep
Selected by C. D. Wright

Severance Songs by Joshua Corey
Selected by Ilya Kaminsky

After Urgency by Rusty Morrison
Selected by Jane Hirshfield

domina Un/ blued by Ruth Ellen Kocher
Selected by Lynn Emanuel

Into Daylight by Jeffrey Harrison
Selected by Tom Sleigh

The Well Speaks of Its Own Poison by Maggie Smith
Selected by Kimiko Hahn

One Hundred Hungers by Lauren Camp
Selected by David Wojahn

ALMOST HUMAN

THOMAS CENTOLELLA

T|P

TUPELO PRESS
North Adams, Massachusetts

Library of Congress Cataloging-in-Publication Data

Names: Centolella, Thomas, author.
Title: Almost human / Thomas Centolella.
Description: North Adams, Massachusetts : Tupelo Press, [2017] | Includes
    bibliographical references. | The Dorset Prize.
Identifiers: LCCN 2017014793 | ISBN 9781936797974 (pbk. original : alk. paper)
Classification: LCC PS3553.E65 A6 2017 | DDC 811/.54—dc23

Cover and text designed and composed in Trade Gothic and Garamond by Howard Klein.
Cover: Photograph by Eric Cahan, "Two Mile Hollow, NY: Sunset 7:22 pm," from
the *Sky Series* (40.9561452, -72.1595295). Used with permission of the artist (http://
ericcahan.com).

First edition: July 2017.

Tupelo Press
P.O. Box 1767, North Adams, Massachusetts 01247
(413) 664–9611 / editor@tupelopress.org / www.tupelopress.org

Tupelo Press is an award-winning independent literary press that publishes fine fiction,
nonfiction, and poetry in books that are a joy to hold as well as read. Tupelo Press is
a registered 501(c)(3) nonprofit organization, and we rely on public support to carry
out our mission of publishing extraordinary work that may be outside the realm of the
large commercial publishers. Financial donations are welcome and are tax deductible.

*"We are not human beings having a spiritual experience.
We are spiritual beings having a human experience."*
— attributed to Pierre Teilhard de Chardin

Contents

I

II

III

IV

V

I

Virgo A

I live on a planet of one.
The storm door, as the meteorologists say, is open,
but the welcome mat, though sodden, is still out.
You might find the view to your liking: what you call the world
is a black and blue fare-thee-well. If you want
I can show you the mango grove, egrets in the lagoon,
I can show you my collection of hand-written scherzi
from a consumptive who died young. Pay no mind
to my mind, it twists like a vine of grapes.
For fun—tell me again what's meant by fun?
It's been a long time. The rumors are true:
I carry the clueless like a bad debt.
My reward: dominion over the invisible.
True or false: This year's genius is next year's joke;
the stricken sky fell and your leader sat still;
people dismiss the probable at their own peril.
Item 1 on today's to-do list: Design a subtle revolution.
What I wouldn't give to consult with someone pure
as the driven snow. Slowly, I am learning the art
of caring from afar. And I'm auditioning new mottoes.
"Wait till next year" isn't one of them.

The Secret Life

It happens on an airplane, a bus, a subway car, a foreign train,
even in the theater before the previews come on or the house lights go down,
before some writer—acclaimed and famous, or whose name
you've never heard before—starts in with a startling examination
of the secret life you can't easily articulate to yourself
and half the time are glad you can't. But before any of that happens
you're out in the unpredictable world, and some woman or man
is close enough to touch, or at least study with impunity,
and what binds you like a spell is something like the *symmetria*
of Polyclitus: a face so pre-possessing, so proportionate and marble-smooth,
at first you can endure it only in its particulars—
the bridge of the nose, the ripple of a lip, how perfectly
each brow crowns each mesmerizing eye. At the Louvre one day
Rilke saw the ruin of a youth he assumed was Apollo—a radiant torso
sans head or arms or legs—and it was enough to remind him
of his limitations: he had to change his life. So imagine how it is
when a breathing divinity is close at hand, oblivious
to your helpless scrutiny, reading a magazine, or staring down
the blank screen of a phone. Who in the world would keep beauty
waiting? Someone who doesn't care for a world
where beauty is an unopposed tyranny. Someone on the fringe
of the fans who purr over the currently designated idol,
gushing that they would do anything for him, for her, anything
at all—someone who remembers that "fan" is short for "fanatic"
and would rather worship an unblemished wall. To look
and not desire, that's the trick—one that Rilke himself aspired to,
though late in his short life, the leukemia like a fire
burning out his will, he was forced to admit
he had done nothing *but* desire. A few more moments
and her stop arrives, or he gives up his seat and moves to the back,
or the house lights go down ... And soon enough
there you are, your face by Picasso, your body by Giacometti

or Renoir, walking into a room that has been waiting for you,
someone says hello, someone you know too well
or not well enough—or nothing but the faces of the hour
greeting your uncelebrated face—and you settle into your chair
or couch or bed, unchanged from the day before, and the day before that,
with the rest of your life staring back at you.

The City

It was a city less famous than infamous
and I took it in like an innocent.
I took in its theatrical statues, its tireless trains,
the sand imported to the edge of its river
so the locals could pretend they were spending
a day at the beach. And of course the imposing house
of politicians, its cupola enormous, home to a dark spiral
which from a distance looked like a tornado
under glass. It took me a while
to notice that the nothing streets I walked
on my way to play Brahms were punctuated
with plaques of clear plastic, a transparency as if to hide
the facts that described, in the minutest words,
a former nerve center of terror. It was a city dead set
on forgetting its shameful aberrations, and I figured
it wouldn't mind swapping its notoriety
for my anonymity. Was that why its citizens
were happy to give me directions, join me
for a drink, slide over at a sidewalk table
where the good food and spirits and my bonhomie
let them believe their city would live forever?
Was that why I was the one later
who would recall everything the city
was loath to admit? Later, alone,
when conversation couldn't keep me
from looking past the couples in the park,
the tourists lounging by monuments, the latest
artful triumph of engineering over memory.
Wherever I wandered there were certain reminders
of the city within the city: a guarded house of worship
half in ruins, bullet holes in a wall
of the shopping district, the cemetery with a solitary

marker, rimmed with stones by those who remembered,
who had no choice but to remember.
And lodged among the cobblestones, a brick
of brass engraved with a woman's name,
the same two words that had spelled out the sentence
of her death. I wondered if there was a corner
where the Big Bad Wolf didn't lie in wait,
and a physicist still played the violin while believing
in a cosmic intelligence, and a writer regarded art
not as a mirror held up to reality
but as a hammer to shape it. I wondered
and I wandered, and then I was entering the hush
of a great temple (though not a temple as such)
where Moses gazed off into the uncertain
future, and Jacob succumbed to an angel in a slip
who seemed to be embracing him tenderly
between her legs, and the winsome Old Master himself
with his moustache and soul patch, velvet hat floppy
on his middle-aged head, a giddy waitress nearly tumbling
into his plump lap, raised a mug of amber ale
in my direction ... I felt the city sigh then,
not so much from yearning as from relief,
a city said to be evil, holy, shining, eternal,
a plexus of animus and genius, renowned for its ravishments—
the Möbius-strip history of the barbaric and the rapturous
hovering like a halo over the heads
of conquerors and savants and laborers—a city in love
with second chances, that meant to defy the ungodly
odds, that would never say die. A city
that wasn't me, but could be.

Attachés

Yes, it has been a long strange trip
and the longer it's gone on the stranger it's gotten.
Why shouldn't we have scoffed at the shameless hussy
who claimed she'd been "severely manhandled on the island of Tobago"—
when she was reading her "victimhood" badly
from a cue card off camera? Remember
that pizza joint on the Upper West Side
where the naturalized counter man was convinced
we were repeat customers, and when we assured him
we weren't, he told us it was good luck to appear
so familiar? It would have been wretched luck
to have disagreed. By the way, this apple juice
is a godsend. And yes, the caramel-filled bon mots
are for sharing, as is this sudden flurry of snow
over that yellow bridge. Can we not use the drive-thru
window at the gentlemen's club and say we did?
First one through customs without crying
gets to keep their sandwich of Bavarian ham.
Which of the multiple languages we're fluent in
do you think will seal the accord?
And are we there yet?

Vermeer: Woman in Blue Reading a Letter

At the Rijksmuseum, Amsterdam

What better way to beat the rain
than to float through the galleries
of imperishable sunlight? Whoever you are
with your damp mane, your coat
like the sky over Delft,

from now on you're the Woman in Blue
Watching the Woman in Blue
Reading a Letter. It might not be true
but it seems you know what the message says:

it's put you in a trance,
a kind of total immersion,
while the less knowing idle by,
murmur their comments, drift off
to their next diversion.

The letter says he's not coming back.
He has his reasons. There are always reasons,
aren't there? They make sense—
call them reasonable—even if
they're far from fair. Your stillness

seems to say you know as much.
You're unmoving as the woman
whose distress hasn't faded
in hundreds of years. She looks—
what would you guess—seven months

gone? Eight? You can feel that other life
inside her kick its sharp reminder

while her stamina dissolves in the blur
of indelible words on indelible paper
she holds in a death grip,

the blue chairs tall and stiff, like servants
who are privy to their master's affairs
and keep quiet, the southern exposure
so merciless you can almost see
the trembling of her young lip...

It's your lip, isn't it? And the sun
that stuns her room floods your own.
The same sun. On the wall behind her,
a map of the Old World. And on both
your faces, a map of the new one.

Pergamon

The museum greeter, perky pretty, suggests I "Carpe diem!"
Easy to do when the day seizes you: half an intact temple rises
step by marble step toward the skylighted ceiling, an "altar"
erected by Eumenes the Second in his quest to create another Athens.
Not yet forty, still reeling from the latest assassination attempt,
his inscription to the gods reads, "In gratitude to good deeds."
In the next gallery an athlete by Daidalos is so lifelike
I can believe the legend that says he had to tie down his statues
to keep them from fleeing. Anchored in her own room—
not that she seems to mind—a woman of dusky rose,
of wide-eyed wonder, holds a small fruit over her stone womb,
and nobody knows: Is she Persephone? Or someone's smiling wife,
smiling mother, enjoying the secret of her immortality?
Yellow lions in a procession of tiles escort me to Ishtar's Babylonian gate
but no farther. The numinous will have to wait. I'll take Assyria's
winged lions, with their human heads, bearded and turbaned, their noses
curved like the Fertile Crescent: in the throne room of red
and gold, I am their lost king. But I'm not Sa'di of Shiraz,
"the poet of the rose garden": too many thorns, not enough grape juice.
And the merchant of Aleppo is four centuries dead. Too bad:
I could use some lamb and couscous. I could use more of this daily bread.

Counterpoint

We do not remember days, we
remember moments.
            —Cesare Pavese

I remember, when we met, she reminded me of a *kore* in an empty temple, her skirt long and slim, eyes like large almonds, subtle smile. A face for the ages, a pure face.

I remember how smooth his hand was when the principal introduced us, and how long it took us to let go.

During the tour of the building she seemed to study me while I told her about the Sumerians setting up the first school rooms.

He complimented me on my earrings—"very Fertile Crescent," he said—and I noticed the tiny hole, no more than a pinprick, in his left ear lobe.

I remember she sat on the floor with the children, who were quieter than usual and kept looking over at her, and who could blame them.

I remember how wonderful he was with the young ones, patient and funny, praising them as if *they* were inspiring *him,* and not the other way around.

In the ancient gym, the kids gone home for the day, she rested her head against the battered upright and asked me to play something sad.

He wanted to know if that was how I felt and I didn't hesitate to tell him.

I remember I was sad myself but too happy to care.

He played the way he taught: *con brio, con amore.*

She recognized the tune and started to sing and joining her I recognized a familiarity—you could even call it a kinship—which I knew was absurd and not a little dangerous, not that it stopped me.

It was a little tense at first, reaching for the high notes, but then how good it felt hitting them, and I remember thinking: I just met this man and feel like I've known him forever.

I remember playing without thinking; only later did it occur to me what all those hours of practice had been for, hours alone with melody, with tempo and touch.

When, on the way to the car, I mentioned my fiancé, he smiled and said, "Well, there's a shocker."

I remember the cold rain and that her compact car felt like a warm cave.

I told him I wanted him to hear this singer I had just discovered, which was true, but really it was because I didn't want him to leave just yet.

While the music played she took off her glasses and looked at me, and I remembered that the eyes of the temple figures had been made large on purpose, to approximate awe in the god's presence.

I don't know if he wanted to kiss me, but he didn't move his eyes from mine, he didn't move at all.

She was leaning slightly toward me and her black sweater made the color of her eyes more compelling, and I wanted desperately to touch her in some way, but the god was unyielding and held me firmly in place.

He was so well-behaved I was aching to kiss him, though I knew I shouldn't.

The song ended and then it was just the rain and its solitary syncopation.

I remember thinking: Knowing this man is going to change my life.

I remember thinking: Knowing this woman is going to change my life.

I went home to my fiancé and told him how happy I was at this new school.

I went home to my piano, my dark altar, and meditated on a song she would later name "Two Angels."

Once, on a warm day in the park, we walked in our bare feet down a long meadow, the astonishing green of it—he kiddingly called it the Garden of Eden—and I remember swallows swooping down to precede us like escorts, the air as pure as it had ever been, and the sense that everything was perfect, in its place, everything was as it was meant to be.

The day we met, later, in the garden, the apples—the burnt orange of the Gravensteins—were wet beneath the dripping branches, and the dog was hypnotized by a supple yellow stripe in the manna grass, and dragonflies skimmed the pond, wings and water playing off each other's glimmer, and I remember how I couldn't tell where my own light ended and the garden's began . . . But all the days of fascination we were given, and later the days of dismay, I don't remember.

II

Nuptial

I claim the mole above your absurdly kissable lips
as a blow against the politically correct.
Likewise the lonely freckle of your *mons veneris,*
which, contrary to a certain popular rant,
I do not prefer shaved so as to incite
the plundering of a prepubescent innocence.
I don't do well with cant, or presumptions
of my predilections, and anyway much of my delight
I find in yours. So if utter nakedness—the smooth
and glide of it, the impulse to unhide—
is your preference, who am I to argue
otherwise? And if it's your wish
that I wrap your hair like a silken rope
around my recent development
so that your face is tethered to my desire
and ncither of us can escape the other,
who should demand we cease and desist?
With all the lethal tensions mounting
by the hour, why not one that brings us to the edge
of a little death that doesn't destroy so much as refresh?
So here's to the new vows: you tell me to claim you. I do.

All That We Think, We Are

My name is Siddhartha and I've never heard of a Noble Truth
or the Eightfold Path. What I know is the keening pleasure
of my goddess wife when I polish the pink jewel of her *yoni*,
and the cooing pleasure of my gorgeous son. All I know
is the palace life: white umbrellas, unguents from Banaras,
silver ornaments to festoon the elephants. The braided hair
of the dancing girls circulates a perfume potent as opium
and I'm inspired to engage in "The Sporting of a Sparrow,"
"The Black Bee," "White Tiger Mounting from Behind"—
with or without my goddess wife. So when I sneak past
the guards one day, I'm captivated by the begging bowl,
the blackened teeth, the creeping lesion. Fascinated
by the child amputee and the frenzy of flies attending
the corpse-bloat by the roadside. Let the flutes of Nepal
sound an eerie tremolo—I feel like shaving my head,
dressing in rags, repairing to the woods, and living on
six grains of rice a day. And swapping one hunger for another
nearly kills me... Wisdom has no use for preconceptions
of wisdom, it simply waits for you to arrive. Once I arrived
I saw that had there been another enticement as great as sex
I wouldn't have begun to learn how to change the world.

Meadow

"This bench," she says, "is better than my bed."
She must mean she feels more rested here—
she's been getting little sleep. It's her brain,
it won't shut off. Then when she needs it to,
the damn thing won't give her the time of day.
But this bench, the tall trees, the sun on her hands—
it's a day, after all. She thinks your retriever agrees,
the swinging tail, muscles on full alert,
and when he springs into a sprint, chasing
something you know won't be captured,
you don't interrupt her excitement. The student
of philosophy you used to be has matriculated
beyond the sweet provocation of words.
The will to power . . . What doesn't kill us
makes us stronger . . . In the end even Nietzsche's brain
was turned against him: the vicious spirochete,
invisible, implacable, boring holes in the magnificence
of his assertions. You don't know how much longer she has—
or you have, for that matter. The bench, the meadow, the trees so tall
they've reached the sun, the dog returning with empty mouth
but glittering eyes—she's right. It's a day, after all.

The Soul

When it was over, or nearly over,
we drove past horses and under banking raptors
and climbed three flights of an empty building
until we reached the attic.

The light was humming in from the west,
the heat smelled immortal.
We could see, down the road, the beach,
a silver thread of surf.
When we turned away

our shadows poured down the ancient floorboards.
On the wall, one of Blake's good angels
holding a child just out of reach
from an evil angel, and the words:
Man has no Body distinct from his Soul.

Suddenly a fluttering above our heads—

a couple of bats, disturbed from their nap.
And on the floor, a thin mattress.
She nodded toward it, her signal
that we could do for each other, once more,
what no one else could do for us.

Would you think us naïve, or maybe given
to narcissism, if I told you we believed
neither of our bodies was distinct
from either of our souls?

She was waiting for me to move.
Her yellow dress, my favorite,
already had slipped to the floor.

This would be, we both knew, the last time.

To this day I don't know what came over me.
"Tell you what," I said, "let's flip for it.
Heads, we do. Tails, we don't."

I flicked a coin at her naked feet.
It must have struck something
like an old groove—it spun,
slender and bright as the soul.

I can still feel the light whirling in place.

Why I'm in Awe of the Spiral

When, in the science museum, I arrive at the overview
of our galaxy, with its tiny arrow pointing to *You are here*
(which really ought to be *We are here*), and see
that the two to four hundred billion stars of our local cluster
are drifting or chasing or dreaming after each other
in circles within milky circles, I can't help but think

of those ancient paintings and rock engravings,
discovered all over our celestial body,
of that one line which begins at whatever point
it can, then curls outward, or inward, toward nothing
anyone can define—the oldest shape revered
by Aborigine and Celt, by mathematician

and engineer and Burning Man reveler alike,
and even accorded a place of honor among the mess
of thoughts on my desk, as a nifty paper clip of copper.
But it's already there in the florets of the sunflower
crisscrossing with the precision of a logarithm,
and in the pin-wheel shape of the Nautilus shell,

and in the coiling neurons of the cochlea
that let us tell Art Tatum from a three-year-old's improvisation.
Call it what you will—"God's fingerprint," "the soul
unfolding through time," "the passageway into the Self"—
I can't help but admire, even fear, something as mundane
as a flush of the toilet, when its swirling is a variation

on our sidereal drift, our existential pain.
And then there's that famous falcon, "turning and turning
in a widening gyre," a portentous symbol of our own
circling into some dread, some pernicious chaos

we thought we had just escaped, one town burning
a decade behind us, a millennium before that,

and into next week, next year, next whenever.
And when the two of us took that winding road
an infinity of others had wound down before us
and would wind down again, our spirits hushed
by the crosses and bouquets at each dead man's curve
and just burning in the dry heat to touch each other,

wasn't that a wondrous and terrible turning?

Ave Maria

Have you ever loved someone deeply, but were allowed to do so
only in scarce moments, though each moment tried its best
to convince you it was made to last, until
against your better judgment you came to believe it?
Then each moment proceeding to the day when all you're feeling
is the absence of that someone, with many days
to follow, many months, then years, until it seems
you have lived through lifetimes with this dispossession,
this deprivation—or maybe, as Nietzsche said, just one lifetime
in which you have died many times—have you ever loved
anyone like that? So that one day you're a foreigner
in a foreign city—Berlin, say, well after the Wall has fallen,
but the park is still there where the hunted would run, briefly,
for their lives, and the angel of victory spreads her two gold wings
on a pedestal above the circling traffic of the centuries.
And across town, in a courtyard on the island of museums,
the even more ancient: a pharaoh sitting on a granite throne
etched with outsized dragonflies (your favorite winged allies)
and many suns, rising and falling on many lives, all of which
reminds you of the eternal that you are lacking, and wishing
you could forget. And if that weren't enough, you follow
the boulevard of lindens to the Brandenburg Gate, where the goddess
of peace steers her sculptured chariot just down the street
from more granite: slabs of various gray, like gravestones,
unmarked, staggered in size, but each one huge—a monument
to the Jewish dead. Say the one you loved was Jewish.
Grief and peace just a block apart. It's enough to keep you
standing stone-still in the August rain. Say August
is the month of your birthdays, and maybe this is the year
you'll be born again in a way you never have been before.
The rain turns to hail but they won't let you take cover
in the elegant hotel—you're not a guest. Which is nothing

but the obvious re-asserting itself: you haven't felt like a guest
for a dynasty or two. So you find the entrance to the underground
and descend again: down into a tunnel of white tiles
that amplify a violin, which is playing of all things
the one song your love promised to sing for you
and never did. A tune that has tracked every one
of your feckless attempts to find in other moments
what you felt one night, half-aware in the bygone
grandeur of a quaint hotel. A night that would always be
sultry, a late summer that would never quite fade
(just as those moments had persuaded you, remember?),
the two of you lying down like acolytes at the altar
of incandescent longing ... Now the music shimmers
toward its conclusion, it doubles itself beneath the earth,
that melody favored at weddings and funerals alike
and which should be crushing you right now.
You should be crumpling to your knees,
not walking away like someone who has a train to catch.
Maybe this is that moment you've always heard about,
the one that could kill you but prefers to make you stronger.
Even though this is a song that never gave up on finding you
through all those days of affection and its afflictions,
all those lifetimes of cursing the gods that decreed
you should know just enough of passion and solace
to believe you would never be yourself without them.

Namaste

The god in me does not honor
the god in you. The god in you
murdered me once, and once
was more than enough.
So the god in me, adept
at keeping my nature warm
and inspired to love the benign,
now prefers the chilly air
of indifference, something picked up
like a virus from the most vicious
of mortals. The god in me
regards the god in you
as suspect, though sad
to say, it wasn't always so.
There were the generous days
in the beginning, when every word
was made flesh. In the beginning
the gods in us were content
to let us go on
behaving like perfect mortals,
which is to say imperfectly,
which is to say with our tenderness
fully intact: the good kind
that let us gladly undress
our trepidations, and pleasure
our solitude into a blissful
oblivion; and the bad kind—
invisible woundings
no compliment or hot kiss,
no confession of the amorous
could soothe for long.

And then, when the mortals we were
had done enough to remind us
that to be mortal is to be susceptible
to the secret agenda, the cruel caprice,
the soft but eviscerating voice—
"at the mercy of a nuance"—
the god in you decided it was time
to act. A dark god, in need
of a human sacrifice, smoothly turning your back
on the earnest and their pathetic pleas.
So the god in me, no stranger to the aberrant
and the abhorrent, now has no choice
but to respond in kind. A pity, really,
since it has been the dream
of so many gods to find themselves
in some quiet room, the burden of power
slipped off and scattered
like clothes across the floor, the light
of late afternoon a kind of benediction,
and everywhere the gratitude
for the privilege of feeling
almost human.

Touching

I don't know what it's for anymore.

Watching these others through my alien eyes
a vestigial feeling flickers.
Certain words, beautiful and familiar,
emerge from the dark:

silken   epithelial   frisson

Topographies I recall from a lucent planet.
Limbs, or are they tentacles, lovely in their entangling.
Appendages, protuberances, fascinating cavities—
all designed, it seems, for some common good,

though the fact that they exist at all
seems anything but common: a spectacle
of texture and form and gesture
in concert with some meaning
to which I don't have a clue.

serotonin   oxytocin   honey pie

And consider the youngest ones, contacted lightly
on the head or shoulder, or energetically embraced.
Why do some recoil, while others seem driven
to be the cherished object of affection?

baby   darling   sweetheart

Lips on cheeks, on foreheads and necks,
lips on eyelids and earlobes and bare throats,
lips on lips giving way to what must be tongues

and the sampling of flavors *hither and yon* ...

Or is this more than mere pleasure?
Is this some kind of ritual:
the moment consecrated, the wounding past
obliterated, the offering of a promise
that this dream of communion,
singular as it seems,
won't be the last?

Angels we have heard on high

Is that what they are. Mortal angels.
Then why wouldn't they be sweetly singing,
creatures of mutual bliss, transporting each other
an eternity from that other world

whose eyes someday will look right through them,
whose memory will contain no record of their names,

while they extend their hands
through the cool, insubstantial air
in the touching belief that they still exist.

III

Orange Alert Creeping into Red

What I wanted was a brain, a heart, and courage,
and what I got was the shock and awe
of a dumbass fumbling behind the curtain
of imminent threat. I wanted to bring back Harold Arlen
to teach inspiration at the University of the Genuine,
and I wanted an all-natural, non-synthesized,
cost-effective, readily available, and gleefully affordable
anodyne for all optimists undermined by manic depression.
What I got was a Yemeni in short sleeves and khakis
sitting on the sidewalk with a pepperoni slice,
flanked by two sturdy suitcases, one of them
yellow as the taxi from the airport there's no way he could afford.
I wanted the peace that passeth all understanding, and what I got
was an axis of evil, tax cuts for the entitled, susceptible levees,
and the stunning tenth-grader waiting for a streetcar named For Hire
who when asked where she was going replied, "An appointment,"
the look from her mascara'd eyes too knowing. I wanted alliances
and allegiances, and what I got was a suspicion of pathogens
simmering in the Yemeni's Samsonite. What I got was a Paiute elder
at the free clinic who said, "Stay calm. Be brave. Wait for signs."
OK, wisdom keeper. And if the signs don't come? "Then that's a sign."

Report on 8275254

Inmate resides in three dimensions:
9, 10 and 11

Age: indeterminate—
young, old, and in between

Domicile on active fault line
above many stone steps

Some moss on the stone
a snail or two (not edible)

So far, no major disasters
So far

Inmate sleeps until the sun arrives
slips from dream as from another room
sprawls across the bed like a body at a crime scene

Rises reluctantly as a ghost
in love with its grave

Iritis in both eyes
arthritis in both knees
but will walk almost anywhere

GPS chip in left arm intact
Inmate can run but can't hide

Can pray but prefers to read
or play a piano
long out of tune

Won't speak to anyone before noon
but when asked for directions
will engage a stranger at length

No tattoos
A solitary piercing
old, healed over,
nearly negligible

Inmate without a mate,
next of kin distant, friends dispersed
or close by but preoccupied

Regards television as a palliative
soothed by how each story
follows the logic of its arc

Consumes red wine daily
for health of the heart ("Valpolicella")
and the occasional "chicken cacciatore"

Regards a self-made meal as a ritual
an athletic move as more art than science
a shower as meditation
whether indoors or out

Presents with Autoimmune Mystery 0702
Has blood tested every three months
Receives therapy weekly in a small movie theater
Current diagnosis: remission through cinema

Not friendly toward PDAs
and their pawns, the brain-washed
who are ignorant of fellow citizens

Doesn't answer surveys
in the street, online, or in the mail
Interrupts telemarketers
but with a modicum of politeness

Had to instruct rookie police
to take note of each detail
of a recent breaking and entering
so he could get back to sleep

Has ceased poring over old images
especially the animated nudes

Has little faith in good will
or the pure gift or the reliable ally
Has little time for fear

Doesn't know how it got to be so late so soon

Doesn't seem to care

The Lost Coast

for Galen Rowell
(1940–2002)

When the winter solstice came and went
and my steady watch went with it, I didn't mind
becoming a fugitive from ticktock routine.
I told time by the presence of light. Sun
gilding the curtains: get up and go to work.
The sky without luster: call it a day.
All day, on my way to anywhere
I had to be, I was running late
or early, or was a poster child for the punctual—
I wouldn't know until I got there.
And when the calendar in the kitchen
ran out of months, the new year joined my watch
in a celebration of independence, free at last
from the obligations of work and play, from appointments
and disappointments. How did that feel, the driven asked me,
leaning in like children eager for a treat. But articulation
had gone on vacation, and couldn't be reached.
At my kitchen table I dreamed over a picture
of the December behind me: the black rocks off the black cliffs
of the Lost Coast, half-drowned in a cobalt swirl of mist,
no sun, no moon, where no one but myself would find me.

The Hope I Know

doesn't come with feathers.
It lives in flip-flops and, in cold weather,
a hooded sweatshirt, like a heavyweight
in training, or a monk who has taken
a half-hearted vow of perseverance.
It only has half a heart, the hope I know.
The other half it flings to every stalking hurt.
It wears a poker face, quietly reciting
the laws of probability, and gladly
takes a back seat to faith and love,
it's that many times removed
from when it had youth on its side
and beauty. Half the world wishes
to stay as it is, half to become
whatever it can dream,
while the hope I know struggles
to keep its eyes open and its mind
from combing an unpeopled beach.
Congregations sway and croon,
constituents vote across their party line,
rescue parties wait for a break
in the weather. And who goes to sleep
with a prayer on the lips or half a smile
knows some kind of hope.
Though not the hope I know,
which slinks from dream to dream
without ID or ally, traveling best at night,
keeping to the back roads and the shadows,
approaching the radiant city
without ever quite arriving.

The Mission

Moving out of my dream cottage in the Mission
I was on a mission: *Travel light.* Not only leave
the burdensome behind—a cumbersome couch, a footlocker
of old letters—but something a stranger would find
a serendipitous delight. That last warm night
no sooner had I cluttered the curb with my former lives
than the boys who spoke nothing but Spanish
came swarming like worker bees to a wild field.
When they brightened over my basketball, or the functioning
TV—no matter that it was black and white—
whose satisfaction was greater, theirs or mine?
Now I wonder in whose cramped and overpriced room
my indigo couch is spread like a spectacular bruise.
Who took home the olive shirt with the epaulettes
and now wears it as if he's a comandante
destined to quit the taqueria and make history?
And what feckless soul, broke beyond broke, bent over
my letter-nest of romance—imploring the mother of God
to let this be some kind of treasure chest—only to recoil
from the sweet stink of mold: an archive of soaring hopes that fell
under the spell of the bittersweet, that other kind of poverty?

Simulacrum

What if the time has come,
time to admit
you are only a simulacrum
of the creature you always wanted
to be, a slight semblance of the one
whom a few occasionally recognized
and in their sincere way praised,
even, sometimes, idolized? Time to admit
that though you were relieved
at having been taken for one of the enlightened,
you've come to believe
your flaws are immutable, a law unto themselves?

And what if your better nature
found its startling counterpart,
but circumstance had other plans
for the two of you, so that now
every unremarkable year
seems a palimpsest of the best ones
before it? What if you've gone
from vivid motion picture
to blurred photograph
and don't even know it,
a phantasm still in love
with the phenomenal?

And what if you spent half the night
walking the shrouded border
between this life and the one after,
remembering the voice in the dream
that told you it was time to take
the next road to being,

but all you could find was a cold bench
on the green patch across from the cathedral
where another being on another bench
was grumbling to his private god,
and you wondered if you were eavesdropping
on yourself, and then

you thought of the one who could always
read your thoughts, and more?
What if your cold eye took in that naked nymph
in the fountain, and the pepper trees,
and the shallow steps leading up to a door
of faux gold, a round window
stained to be stunning—and you were stunned
by that time you sat with your better nature
in the dark choir loft in the heart
of the day, like a couple of blissed-out visitors
just arrived on earth, kissing your way
into existence, and now

it's time to go back to whatever
remorseless force sent you here,
but not before you had your final say?
What if it's time to come clean and admit
the best you will ever be has already happened,
that the manuscript is erasing itself,
the illuminations fading without provocation,
but there are still a few crucial words
you need to invoke,
the ones that still soothe
even as they scathe, that still hold
their mystery close, though they've been mindlessly stripped

of meaning—what if you could summon the last
of your charms, the ones admired by the well-intentioned,

and then consider the unconscionable, those masters
of blandishment and betrayal, who cast too cold an eye
on life, on death—on your life, your death—
what if you could wave your hand and all was forgiven,
or at the very least forgotten, a forbearance, a largesse
it wouldn't even occur to them to want from you?
Do you think that would save you from the cheap days
of defeat, that it would be enough to keep you here
a while longer, as if you had a critical mission to complete?
Whether or not you believed in purpose.
Whether or not there was anyone left
who believed in you.

Renunciation

It took some time, but I've given up on giddy Yes
to embrace her sober sister, No. Doesn't matter
what the street signs say, every road now
is the *via negativa*. Yes can go on
wearing her little black dress, whisper
how much she's missed me, giggle
at our running jokes—I'm shaking my head,
I'm holding up one hand like a crossing guard,
like a saint inhabiting a stone niche
while the faithful count their current blessings,
no matter how meager or mundane.
I agree it smells sweet, the fragrance
of a second chance, the seductive whiff
of the would-be. But this is the yes
of a fifth chance, a tenth chance,
a last chance. This is that siren-voice
cooing no to my no, the same voice that once
dismissed my yes without consideration,
much less compassion. I thought compassion
was always the way to go. Was I right?
No, no, and no.

Loneliness

Well before the winter solstice:
light in short supply,
a serrated chill in the air.

For example, my beautiful neighbor.
Passing me on the street or in the aisle
of our local grocery, she made certain
her eyes stayed trained on some
distant target of oblivion.

A middle-aged man at the magazine stand
scanning the glossy pages
of unclothed gods and goddesses,
a scavenger through the remnants
of the sacramental.

The moon came up early, a pale orange
imported from Valencia.

And a black sedan, askew in its driveway,
the light on inside, a woman sitting so still
she had all the affect of a mannequin.

It seemed I lived in a city of the dead.

Of course it could have been
I was projecting like a madman.

I fell asleep to water gourd and kalimba
and woke to the hopeless cries
of two beings attempting
to become one.

And I made certain to wear every day
my beaded bracelet from the Masai.
Told the schoolchildren
I was a warrior. Some of them
even believed me.

Once again our space station
was in need of repair. So why
wasn't I assigned the mission?

Pundits of politics, gurus of self-help—
I listened, but not for long, as they wallowed
in the muddy excrement of metaphor.

And in the auditoriums and art galleries and bookstores
the poets with their unlined faces
and graduate degrees held forth
like proud prophets of the god Abstraction.

A shortage of power
and dire predictions. Blackouts
rolling across the state. Why then
wasn't I consulted?

Some professed their love
only when it was convenient,
a kind of selective affection.

On the bus, a guitar yellow as a pear
played the distance between
one faint star and the next.

Once again I was invisible to the rulers of the planet.
Only children and animals could see me,
only they had the power to pull me close.

Somebody crossing the city on foot,
trying to live the myth of one
who has no need to live by myth.

Sometimes the flags atop the four-star hotels
had failed. Sometimes, a languid ripple.

Somebody arriving home, and before going in
looking at where the sun disappears.
Ritual acknowledgment of the evanescent.

Instead of bringing my face into the fragrance
of one who had professed to have my welfare at heart
but now was betrothed to silence,
I would stop for the new rose, loosening
its tight clothes even in early December.

And an upright piano,
dressed in black and white,
heard the daily confession of one
abandoned to naked bitterness.

The latest technology brought communiqués
from the other world. Sometimes, between
the lines, there was something approaching
the authentic—a tone, an inflection—
enough to drift into unconsciousness
on a cloud of belief.

And approaching me in the street
on the shortest day of the year,
a tall creature with long lively hair.
Kept my eyes down until the last
possible moment. And when I looked up—

Beautiful Neighbor, cutting her eyes at me,
rushing by with the startled look
of *Who the fuck are you
and what do you want from me?*

What to make then of the visitation
of a green-eyed inspiration from a world
without irony, who showed me the brazen
naked angel on her shoulder blade,
who insisted that life was good—simple
as that—and tempted me to agree?

Over the western horizon,
light and power in short supply,
look at the pink cirrus—or is it a circus—
entertaining the end-of-the-day mind.

A few moments and it's gone to gray.
A few more and it seems gone for good.

But in all the rooms, no matter the hour,
the Africans never stop singing
of loneliness, and the spirit
that holds it up with care
as if it were a frail elder,

as if it were the very being
that brought our being into this world.

IV

Song

Without music, life would be a mistake.
— Nietzsche

Sometimes all I had in the world was a song.

Because I am an American, most songs at first were American. But as time went on they might be Jamaican, or Irish, or Hungarian. Often they arrived from South America or West Africa or the Middle East in a language I didn't speak but which, translated through its music, spoke to me. A language which itself seemed a kind of song.

A song of complaint, a call to prayer, a wedding song. A rapturous melody from Mexico, bittersweet, like chocolate, to which I would become addicted. A Bulgarian rhapsody, an Italian revelry, a French kiss.

Sometimes the song was one of my own. Though to be honest, I couldn't tell you where it came from or how it got here. Sometimes it would show up as a few beguiling notes, a melodic wisp, when I was far from a piano and tending to the less-than-inspiring business of life. I would have to hum these notes just under my breath, *sotto voce*, over and over, until I could get home, figure them out on my upright, then play out their possibilities into something that might be recognized as a bona fide song.

But sometimes other matters would intrude, and that hint of song, impatient, would vanish, abandoning me for someone who could take it in, give it the proper attention and encouragement. I would have no choice then but to let the song go, a touch wistfully, though not without gratitude for its brief apparition.

For all the songs that left me, there were those that wouldn't leave me alone. Many started out charmingly enough—usually on the radio—only to become vexing as a hex. On the other hand, there were the familiar songs that popped into my cranium like omens, or encrypted messages, which—

once they had my full attention—revealed to me with an unfailing and startling accuracy some old issue or newfound obsession I had been hardly aware of. Maybe that's why songs are written in something called a key. They unlock what is crucial. And in doing so, songs themselves become key, become central, vital.

Like this elegant dark-haired song, glistening with sweat, that has walked to my house all the way from its neighborhood in Havana. Or this crackling blues rant, electric as a Texas thunderstorm.

One night in the chapel at Harvard, I sat in the back row with a friend and listened to a Beethoven piano sonata. One movement had been inspired by children and was directed, I assumed, to all those with like spirit. It certainly had that effect on us—we were seized by a giggle attack. It got to the point where I actually had to bite the heel of my hand. The more the music played, the more we wanted to laugh, the more agitated were the sophisticates in front of us, the less decorum seemed to matter. It was a long-deceased composer, colicky, destitute, with a dour face and deaf ears, now making it known that not only was he not dead, but he had been privy to the eternal need for play, for spirit, for incorruptible joy. And if we were compelled to giggle like a couple of sugar-dosed school kids—well, that was exactly the point, and we had better take advantage, or be doomed to another hour of stupefying propriety. Another hour of ancient elation greeting you—and you too absorbed in doubt and debt and hunger and empire and heartbreak and soulbreak and resentment and poor health and impermanence. Too lost in yourself to hear a song of respite, a drinking song, a dance mix, a love ballad, a chant to the transcendent, a silly ditty without a name.

I have often made my way through the world without a name, scarcely aware of who I was, or who I might become. And all I had to keep me here was a song.

Southerly Wind and Fine Weather

for Evelyn Belvin
(1912–2005)

Jangly jangly down the hilly street.
Damn but my legs feel long today.

It's about time the winter rain grew tired of itself.
It's a Hokusai sky, blue blue, with white clouds, slender,
wide and scalloped: *Southerly Wind and Fine Weather.*

Your hands are cold, I said. You must have a warm—
Don't say it, she said.

Deal.

Speaking of deals, we had agreed: 100 and out.
None of this 92 year old crap.

I tried, she said, but life had other plans,
life always has other plans.
It's a bitch.

The wind's coming now from the west,
a cold affront. Not so fine.

My next birthday, she said,
won't be a birthday,
it'll be an expiration date.

The clouds are moving in on Tiburon like a school of sharks,
big and indifferent, mostly gray.

Having done masterfully all he could do,

Hokusai, 88 years old, shivers inside
his yellow kimono.

Damn but my hands are cold today.

Reps

Why mess with free weights or pulleys or any other contraption
of tension, when each day lends itself to repetition?
A circuit of days, each one determined to outdo
the one before it, each one aiming to please.
You're working out, you could say, but working out
what? Not pectorals but problems, possibly
the problem—whatever the day dictates.
Maybe it's patience: you've run out of it,
you want to cut to the chase, or better yet,
to that face that abducts your attention
from whatever matter is at hand. Like money:
every month you can just cover your rent,
while some ball player jokes about blackjack—
a mere five hours to drop a cool two mil.
The day says you're allowed to vent with a *Fuck that*
and stiff middle finger, but then you need to move along.
The plum trees, pink-petaled, once again are defying
the mandate of February. A single mother takes her time circling
the cathedral's labyrinth, as if dragging a royal mantle. A great kiss, don't forget,
inspires another one. And that ripe orange the Chinese say brings good fortune?
That's the sun.

Creeley
(1926–2005)

Jackhammers. It must be October.

If the man with the black eye patch were still alive
he might pause in his latest digression,
he might turn to the classroom window and murmur,
"A little something for our attention
to work against." He might return
to his reminiscence of two green poets
making another pilgrimage to the Master
of New Jersey. They sit in Dr. Williams's sun room
like two Boy Scouts hankering after a merit badge.
Or he might meditate aloud on the attributes
of Levertov: "Responsibility is the ability
to offer a *response*," fixing the room's fledglings
with his one good eye. Then maybe
another pause, while he digs deep
for his hanky, flips up the pirate patch
and wipes out the moist hollow nobody wants
to look at. Then off he goes again—the time
he and Famous Name went to Famous Place
and took another step toward celebrity—
until, fidgety with tangent and anecdote,
we pull him back on track because,
one day after class, he said he'd go on
and on if nobody stopped him.
We stopped him—when we could.
He would chuckle, which you could say
was his way of being responsible…
A jackhammer shatters the concrete
and I'm staring again at the rheumy cave
of an eye socket. We were good students,

I think. We took on the interruptions
and reinforced our focus.
We looked death in the eye
and didn't blink.

Tonic

Someone more informed than I will argue
it's a mistake to think that sadness
is our keynote. Someone tougher,
who can riffle through the inevitable
the way my father's thumb
riffled the corner of the phone book
after his cousin—his best friend—succumbed
to a heart attack at fifty-eight. The relatives
were trading jokes in the dining room
while in the kitchen my cousin and I
kept my father company, three men standing
with hard liquor in their hands and nothing
much to say. It was obvious that this death
had struck my father an unspeakable blow,
someone with a dicey heart of his own,
obvious that the longer he lived
the more he would outlive the ones
who could help him take the edge off
the most cutting joke of all: we are born
to die. In the bright dining room, another punch line,
another detonation of laughter, while in the dim kitchen
my father studied his own thumb
moving against the sharp pages
of names that were fated to appear, someday,
on memorial stones, and it was as if my cousin and I
were at my father's bedside, watching him go.
Someone more heroic than I
would have vanquished the convenient platitudes,
the custom-made clichés, and crossed
the length of a room that seemed more treacherous
than the sea, and taken my father
by his arm and led him from the weak light

of the too-quiet back into the radiant and the raucous.
Not someone who knew something I didn't,
but who wouldn't care if my father had insisted
on standing his mournful ground. Someone bold enough
to act, whatever the consequences. Twenty-five years later
and my father still plays the fool on the phone,
greeting me with the babble of baby talk,
a cooing falsetto my mother pretends to ignore
but is secretly grateful for, and which I
don't hesitate to answer: a jester and his son
regressing to their private playpen, the music they make
a kind of first language in which nothing grave
need be acknowledged, ludicrous music, pure
gibberish, pure indulgence, and irresistible.

Piano

If I should be grateful
to anyone or anything
I should be grateful to you

How many years of disconsolate hours
have you had something to say
I needed to hear

The masters wake from their genius sleep
and it's your voice that presents their arguments
against demise   against the destined

to be forgotten
the already forgotten
your voice that will rise

as needed
before slipping back
into its bed of silence

A silence composed
of every note ever played
and ever to be played

all the possible permutations
of time sounding
its own depths

the simple key that unlocks a complex secret
the ingenious combination
that opens a treasury

How serene you seem
considering you keep in confidence
everything that has come before

and is still to come
which is why I go to you
for the way forward

even if it means looking back
and though I don't believe
as some do

in salvation
you never fail
oracular wonder

to negotiate the mysterious
union of the divine and the human
playing upon me as you are played

issuing revelations
with a sympathetic vibration
I can't help but feel

will save me

Your Legion

We're writing to let you know we're out here,
believing in the small things
you've taken great pains to remind us of.
Our numbers might be small themselves
but we're loyal, and intent on creating
some critical mass. From the front lines
of a Tennessee highway, a peak
in the San Gabriel Mountains,
a concrete bunker on a lonely campus,
the message is clear: we are one spirit
with many names. Yes, we have sustained
serious losses, decimated by forces
within and beyond us,
have weathered countless assaults
on our esteem, on the burning dreams
of no interest to anyone.
But because of you
we persist in believing
our fate lies in more
than sovereign despair, in something welcome
we can trust. We've heard rumors
that you don't think yourself the visionary
we deserve. We're writing to say
you're doing your best. Whether your best
is good enough for the indifferent world,
we can't say, but it's good enough for us—
we who have no use for the small minds
that mean to make us feel small.
We might never meet face to face
but may you continue to be sustained,
as we are, by this correspondence between us
that confounds the enemy: congenial words

plain enough, but encoded with messages
crucial to our survival. May they remain
our weapons and our rations,
and the small fires that spit
at the bitterest cold, the darkest invasions,
and don't know when to quit.

In the Valley of the Moon

After midnight in the sumptuous wine country
called the Valley of the Moon,

after the killing illness
you outlasted, the doctors stymied
before and after, your alleged friends

ignorant of the danger
or too self-involved to care,

just clear of the horizon
comes a wedge of *la luna*,
a distillate of pale orange,
like a liqueur.

Nothing between you but the abundant
vineyards, nothing above you

but the scintillant beauty
you can't see by day
and must take on faith.

Something like a star whooshes
halfway across the dark.

No need for wishes.

La Purisima

Who knows when you'll encounter royalty?
Unacknowledged queen of green Mulegé,
you were short and plump as a favorite aunt,
presiding over the modesty of your ice cream shop,
our after-dinner respite. We came to you
as two refugees fleeing the land of plenty, impoverished
by the belief we could always do better. We came desperate
for your vanilla bean and the fat-rich chocolate
you churned by hand. Routed by doubt and argument,
we came weary, with few words between us, more worn
than your wooden Mother Mary—and left moaning
over the little homemade raisin cookies
you threw in for free. I still wonder
what you saw in us, if you could see how keenly
in need we were. Or were you this way
with everyone, quiet and generous,
handing over more change than expected?
Something in me wants to believe
you could tell how eager we were to visit you
evening after blue evening, in the muzzy realm
between having and wanting . . . You
our foreign majesty, waving away flies
and our petty threats to the kingdom,
you in whose presence we were defeated
by peace, our gentle eminence, the one
I still bow my head to, the purest one.

The Year

More than fifty Junes
and still I tend to forget:
beneath the blooms—thorns.

*

Rising for incense
a moment after sitting
is meditation.

*

Hate the goddamned wind.
My grocer shows off his kid.
Suddenly, no wind.

*

Cherry branch in hand,
you made the cold night less cold
and spring come early.

V

The Belief Gene

It's the holidays—formerly known as
the holy days—and the creationists
are mud wrestling with the evolutionists.
All I can say is: Thank God for science.
Isn't science the means by which the unknown
reveals itself: the trick behind the magic,
the method in the madness, the design disguised
as the seemingly random? Who doesn't love a good mystery
solved? Now that the geneticist has identified
the iota of me that allows for belief
in much more than me, faith can take a break
from those hazardous leaps, spare the fractured soul
more days in traction. It looks like that fisherman
with the human touch was prescient all along:
heaven *is* a kingdom within us—a wonderment
of DNA that studies itself and every year
has more to say about what it's doing here.
Meanwhile, a block from the Federal Building, a not-so-old
woman in a wheelchair bows her weeping head against the cold
and her empty cup. My VMAT2 gene—slipping her a dollar,
directing me back to the last-minute shoppers—wants to scream.

Jesus Enters the City after Midnight

So the ass is passé, he thinks, but no donkey smells any worse
than this bus of fumes—tobacco and booze and herb,
slept-in sweat, the ammonia of fresh urine.
And who invented these lights, the Dark One?
Bright enough for a lobotomy… Jesus is having a hard time
seeing through a window darkly. All he knows
is that he's heading downtown, no clear plan, a tired man
among the dregs of men. His dwindling "brides"—
and God bless the ones who have hung around—
are scattered all over, attending to the even less fortunate.
Nobody here bothers him with more than a glance:
his reputation might precede him but not his mug.
The Turin shroud was good press for a while
but not a good likeness. His hair has forever
been cropped, close as Caesar's, and his face—
it only feels long. The crown of thorns was a nice touch,
a stand-in for his migraines. Here comes another stink-wave
of warm piss, and a bottle, drained, rattling
down the aisle. What did that street sign say?
Neon's a red smudge, like the mouth of that whore
who could only wobble down the hallway with her hands
on the wall. At least the least of him doesn't lack
a way to stay in touch: every minute or so, a ring tone
that hints of connections if not deliverance—
hip-hop or techno, and is this one a burst of Haydn?
The faithful say he's due for a fantastic comeback,
but he's weary of spectacle: politicians, celebrities, evangelists—
too many of them overrated. He's well on his way,
he thinks, to joining them. His dreams have become
pedestrian: it's always the street, the street, the street
while he searches for a shelter that never closes,
but to everyone he meets he's the shelter

and he can't pull change from his gritty pocket
fast enough. Tonight his last three bucks will deliver him
to Donut World, which anyone here will tell you
might not be rapture but is better than church.
Coffee and crullers over bread and wine: whatever
it takes to resist the desire to lie down on some bench
and not rise for a long time ... That's not Haydn.
It's Handel. Genius spirit, still singing among the stench.

Examination

There is no peace in this body.
Nor in this one. In this body
there is a little peace, and in this one
a bit more, but not much.
In this body there is ample peace
(note the hint of smile), and in that one
as well (the casual arm on the back
of the bench). Now this body here
has great peace, but no breath to speak of.
This one has great breath but no peace.
I have seen a body with calm
and spirit to spare. Colors to rival
the fields of Arles. The diligent clarity
of a Kashmiri sky. But bodies like that
are rare... All right. I need to go home now
and acquire some peace of my own.
When the spirits come to visit they bring
poppy seed cake and their favorite pens
and keep mostly to the corners. At first
I thought they were lonely. Then I realized:
there is no end to what must be learned.

Stranger

What was he: a man, a god,
something stupendously in between?
Neither young nor old, dressed casually
in the style of the day, strolling
through the city square.
The new buildings, he noticed,
asserted themselves against the white sky
but lacked imagination.
Not that anyone seemed to care.
There were treasures to be acquired,
fortunes to be made (or at least
bills to be paid), assignations
in a hotel room the color of ripe papaya.
He saw a young woman
toting a large bag, a pale scar
splitting her pale forehead
like a scimitar, and he thought:
You've had an interesting accident.
At the bus stop a man approached
in a cloud of decay, and though
he wasn't begging for his supper
everyone else stepped away
as from a leper. In an office window
the present was taking the future
to task, and the future was rising
from its dark chair . . .
Was this the world
to which he was best suited,
to which he could deliver
an unforgettable transformation?
What exactly were these people
lacking? Everywhere he went,

a seething, and a restlessness.
Did they suffer from an absence
of what that Guadalajara sorceress
called *cariño,* and a Kyoto monk
called *loving-kindness*? A dearth
of daily affection—was that the empire's
malady? And what could be the cure?
Every other melody sang of romance
or violence, and in any given hour
he could witness a hundred gullible souls
being programmed, their ear pieces
firmly in place. Indifference
arrived on a cold wind,
but a tall palm brought in
from a more temperate climate
modeled its fronds as if the unpleasant air
was of little consequence.
On the other side of the square
elevators rose like angels,
the visitors inside hypnotized
by the view, all their troubles
many time zones away.
Would it matter if he waved,
a little addendum to their pleasure?
Would they even notice?
He looked up at the dark glass,
faces he couldn't see. The sky
was blank, a tabula rasa.
He raised his hand.

Spirit

There was a time when I tried being all things,
if not to all people, then to myself.
I knew that what the world called God
was hunkered down in the battle trench
of the corpus callosum.
I knew how certain men were satisfied
with nothing less than the forcing of their will
on circumstance, that for them
time would always be the enemy
and success the great leveler.
I knew a woman's loveliness
could be ruined for life
by the wrong touch or the wrong time.
And I knew about the best of intentions,
how misguided they could be
and how necessary. I knew secrets
that had survived the sordid rise
and fall of so-called civilizations,
secrets without a text, without rites
or rituals, and I knew animals
were often better off than anyone
strutting on two feet. What I knew
I couldn't always say,
didn't always want to.
I was a genius of dreams,
a reticent guest, the exhausted angel
without blessing or bliss, the friendly
demon that keeps things interesting.
The world called me human
but what was the world?
A shapeshifting, a shimmer,
the latest permutation in a Petri dish.

The world called me human
but I was a sound bite, a statistic,
half-believed lyrics in a dog-eared hymnal,
particles careering through an experimental accelerator,
more ether than matter.
Or, if flesh and bone, then merely
a scorched torso strung up on a bridge
and enough blood to fuel the end of days.
I knew energy was eternal delight,
even for a compromised immune system,
especially for a compromised immune system,
and I despised the despoilers of energy.
I despised anyone and anything
that would deprive a breathing creature
of its rightful inheritance
to health, ecstasy, and peace of mind.
I worked for a living
but never so hard as when I slipped
from one persona into the next
simply to remain among the living.
Whoever claimed in a loud voice to know me
knew only as much as the fates
would permit. Rumors had their run,
then indifference. Regardless
of the pronouncements on my character,
the unceasing projections, I kept my distance.
Whether commanding a stage or nodding off
in the audience, I knew better than anyone
what I was and wasn't,
which I'm sure many would say
isn't saying much. After a while
I learned the error of my ways,
as much a cause for laughter as terror.
After a while I learned what was what
and what was not what.

My time has come and has passed
more times than anyone can remember.
And will come again. In the meantime
I have learned to endure what many cannot:
Godly calm. Ungodly desire.

Remnant Magic

The black cat in Egyptian sitting position
painted on a boulder by the mountain road
landmark for the turn-off to the lake

The unnamed trees so numerous
they crowded the water
no room for a beach

Other than the plash and swoosh
against hull and paddle
the quiet   an unconquerable domain

The way your canoe's bow would rise
on the incidental wave   rise
until earth and water disappeared

and then the nearly fearful
thrill of nothing
but sky

The barren island out of nowhere
that could be traversed
in seven steps

The lush island in the distance
its celadon mist
that seemed too far to reach

Beauty on four elegant legs
grazing on greens at the water's edge
no need to heed the stranger drifting by

You shirtless muscled fearless
the sun beneficent
your guide and companion

The so-called pleasure craft
alluring and hollow
still ages and ages away

Clear across the bedazzling lake
a channel   narrow reedy shallow
that led to another bedazzling lake

And clear across that lake
another channel
another lake

And so on and so on
until it was clear
you were the explorer

who had come to discover
what had only existed in legend
in the imagination's hunger

a world beyond
the world   shining
and without end

Notes

Virgo A
This poem's title refers to the giant elliptical galaxy also known as Messier 87, which is 53.5 million light-years from Earth.

Pergamon
The title is the name of the antiquities museum of Berlin, named after the Turkish town where Eumenes's altar was excavated.

Namaste
The title is a traditional Hindu greeting, roughly translated as "The god in me honors the god in you," and "at the mercy of a nuance" is a quote from E. M. Cioran.

The Lost Coast
Galen Rowell was an acclaimed nature photographer and wilderness lover.

Creeley
Robert Creeley, American poet. "Levertov" is Denise Levertov, American poet and activist (1923–1997).

The Belief Gene
"VMAT2" is pronounced "vee mat too."

Acknowledgments

Thanks to the editors of the following magazines for publishing some of the poems here: *Alaska Quarterly Review*, *Marin Poetry Center Anthology*, *Parthenon West Review*, *Poetry Northwest*, *Third Coast*, and *Washington Square Review*.

"Orange Alert Creeping into Red" first appeared, in a slightly different version, in *Avanti Popolo: Italian-American Writers Sail Beyond Columbus* (ManicD Press, 2008).

Thanks to the Rockridge Group and the Corte Madera Group for their thoughtful responses.

My profound thanks to Carl Dennis for his invaluable help in bringing this book to its final form.

I also owe a debt to Huston Smith and his classic *The World's Religions* (HarperSanFrancisco, first published in 1958) for inspiring parts of this book.

Other Books from Tupelo Press

See our complete list at www.tupelopress.org